REBOOT YOUR CAREER

SANDY CULLEN

Testimonials

"Sandy gave me valuable guidance and insights when I was looking for a new role. [...] For anyone looking for career advice, I don't hesitate in recommending Sandy."
Ricardo Rocha, EMEA Food Manager

"Sandy is an outstanding career coach and communication specialist. If you're looking at a career transition, look no further."
Caroline Brown, IS Business Support Specialist

"In a very difficult market, his counsel and efforts were invaluable and, without a doubt, helped me secure a new role."
Michael Kurtyka, Executive Manager Glasgow School of Arts

"[Sandy's] experience, guidance and advice proved invaluable in many ways, from revamping my CV to make it more attractive, to role playing interviews for specific job roles I was going after. [...] After just 3 consultations with Sandy I found myself with two job offers, [...] it was largely due to Sandy's input that I was able to achieve this and I would highly recommend him to anyone at a career crossroads."
Gerry McColl, Scottish Government Team Manager

"I fully enjoyed working with Sandy and would recommend his services to anyone looking for support in a range of areas."
Sandy Murray, Vocational Educational Manager , North Lanarkshire Council

REBOOT YOUR CAREER

SANDY CULLEN

Baberton
Books

Published in 2022 by Baberton Books

ISBN Paperback: 978-1-7393421-0-4
Ebook: 978-1-7393421-1-1

Illustrations by Georgina Hart

Published with the help of Indie Authors World
www.indieauthorsworld.com

IndieAuthors
World

To my dear sister, Lucy, who died so prematurely.

Contents

Introduction

In 2004, I was working as a freelance financial recruiter when I received a call from a recently redundant finance director. Aged 55, he wanted me to help him to find a new job because he was 'struggling' and getting nowhere with his own efforts. I arranged to meet him and, after chatting for half an hour, I realised that not only did he have a broad range of knowledge, experience, contacts and a list of relevant skills, he was also a thoroughly engaging individual. In short, he was eminently employable.

Sadly, however, the first part of his problem was that he had no idea of how to approach the potential jobs market and, second, his CV was awful – even including his date of birth clearly written at the top (in those days, honesty with such things was seen as the best approach). Having applied for several advertised roles, he'd remained unsuccessful, but couldn't understand why. And changing his method of attack had simply not occurred to him.

But then two things occurred to *me*: a) The last time he'd had to apply for a job was at least 40 years previously and people within his age group (50+) were often overlooked for that reason alone – despite their possibly being ideal for the role and b) He needed help and guidance. But I also realised that there were many people who were similarly challenged, and so I decided to offer career management help, principally to those over 50.

And it was extremely popular.

Choosing London as a fertile proving ground. I started by placing small ads in the *Telegraph* and going there once a week, using an ideally situated serviced office near Victoria. Every client had a different background and personal makeup with which to work but, very much on a one-to-one basis, I adhered closely to my basic principles of a) First of all, define what, actually, is the 'product' you're hoping to market, b) know that people employ *people* and c) that, consequently, a face-to-face meeting is always preferable, if not essential. At that time, I was able to help a great number of people – mostly senior in rank as well as age – to identify, and subsequently exploit, some very good opportunities. And it most certainly was not rocket science. In fact, the most popular phrase I heard then was; "Gosh, Sandy. That's common sense!"

Since 2008, however, and having recognized a more universal need here in Scotland, I've tended to focus my work on people of all ages and experience – from graduates to CEOs, junior staff to managing directors. This book, then, offers basic tips on a range of relevant subjects, setting out in simple terms not only the key principles of career management, but also in office culture and the entire process of how to identify and then to apply successfully for a job. I explain, for example, how to write an *effective* CV and how to produce 'readable' letters easily, how to perform well at interviews and even how to conduct a memorable presentation or to impress them enough to want actually to meet you.

Since the Covid pandemic and lockdown, many working practices have changed and there are those who claim that the standard working week has changed permanently to a 'hybrid' or four-day format. This may well be true, but then the need for people to make the right move is now more important than ever.

My two key messages in this book are: to keep things as simple as possible and to make sure that you can engage fully with the right people and I make no apology for repeating those mantras throughout. It really can work in your favour. But essentially, it's how the art of effective communication can help you to achieve things you'd never even imagined.

Chapter 1

Thinking of changing your Job?
Or even your career…?

It's early morning and you're heading for work. Is this a good feeling, or are you simply looking forward to 'another day at the coalface'? If it's the former, then congratulations, you're one of the lucky few. However, if it's the latter, then at least you can be sure you're not alone. Ask anyone about their job, they'll often say something like: 'Yeah, it's OK; pays the bills…' But real job satisfaction? Hmm.

In fact, many people see this elusive, so-called job satisfaction as simply unattainable. And, actively or passively, these people may be quietly casting around for something better, and if passively, it tends to be more of a sort of '… just in case. Well, you never know…' formula. But reasons for this dissatisfaction can vary enormously. Often, it's just that the job hasn't quite matched the role as presented at interview – nor is it likely to – but can also include: inability to get on with your peer group; poor working conditions; low salary; lack of communication or understanding from mid-senior management; coercive bullying or harassment issues; zero prospects... the list goes on.

But then the issue can simply be one of boredom: you've done the same job (extremely well) for many years and, as such, you can often be relied upon to pick up the tedious donkey work that others are inclined to foist upon you: "Ah, Gladys, would you just check these figures for me? Ta. Yer a star." 'Gladys' may have to work well past her usual leaving hour, but she'll do it. She always does. There's little hope of further promotion and, just like Gladys, the future stretches out in front of you like a road across a desert. You just need a change, or at least something to look forward to every day, every week... every month.

For example, someone I met recently (in his early 50s) was desperately keen for a change. He'd joined a senior bank when he was 16 and following their career advancement programme, he did well, ultimately becoming a director – in charge of a team of 37 and working mostly in Europe, to where he travelled on a regular basis.

Mortgage paid off, three children all self-reliant, a happy situation you might say. But, essentially, he was not only bored but he had hit a 'glass ceiling' and knew he was unlikely to advance further within the bank – and he still had more than 10 years to go... Golly.

So how would you describe job satisfaction? Possibly reaching the end of the working week, looking back and being proud of what you'd achieved? Every week? However, job *dis*satisfaction can simply form part of an unfulfilled desire to develop your career in a different direction and rise to a position of greater responsibility, financial reward or achievement. This requires your superiors (and often your peers) to at least acknowledge your skills and attributes such that they will agree that your promotion is not only right, but possibly (probably) overdue. Good management practice is extremely important here, whereas Management Myopia is often more likely to be much more predominant. The key to gaining any form of promotion is to ensure your efforts are being recognised purely for what they are, and not in a 'Hey! Look at Me!' way. If these efforts remain unrecognised by myopic and unsympathetic seniors, then dissatisfaction in those who are affected is bound to result.

This, then, can be time to take things into your own hands and not simply wait for Fate to play its part. Seeking professional career advice is an obvious start and there are individuals and companies who can help. Another plan is to review your CV, which can be a revealing exercise on its own. Would *you* hire this person? If so, why? Carry out a deep self-assessment of those skills and achievements I referred to earlier. As ever, think of yourself as a 'product' with features and benefits that you're hoping to 'sell' – and make sure you're offering exactly what the market (or your target organisation/individual) is looking for. Meet with as many contacts as possible, as they're the ones who will direct you to an opportunity. Take charge of events.

The issue here is being able not only to recognise the reasons for job dissatisfaction, but also to be aware of the remedy and to put plans into action. Effective networking or using online help (e.g., LinkedIn) can all play a part. It's now up to you to make it happen.

Chapter 2

Redundancy: How to cope – and capitalise...

Being made redundant is likely to be extremely unsettling to anyone and the longer you've been with this employer, the harder it is to bear: 'But why *me* for goodness sake? This just isn't fair!' is an emotion suffered by many as they struggle to cope with the stigma and reality of having, suddenly, no job to go to. 'So this is it, then? Rendered 'Unfit' and, most likely, 'Unemployable'?? Or are you....?

Absolutely not! Assuming you've been with your erstwhile employer for longer than five minutes, your redundancy package will, almost certainly, include a settlement that will offer you the cash equivalent of around, say, 12 weeks' salary/wages. The one cautionary note, though, is that because you are now living outside the employer's protective 'bubble' – in terms of daily costs of living (heat, light, even sustenance) – those three months can pass extremely quickly; and you should beware.

But 'unemployable'? Why? The skills and experience you've developed over the years are not redundant and will still remain attractive to another employer – and not necessarily in the same sector, particularly when you can offer a range of the much sought-after soft skills – like man-management, motivation and profit-awareness. These are 100% *transferable* skills that many employers would give anything for. The same applies to more practical or hands-on skills found, say, in factories or development sites. Or within the hospitality sector, where employers are currently desperate to find both skilled and unskilled operatives right now. Would you consider a role there? Why not research the options at least? You and your skillset will continue to be in demand and you should use this hopefully brief hiatus to use your redundancy settlement wisely.

Many people think that the stigma of redundancy means you'll be forced forever to wear a jacket with: "Was Made Redundant!" stitched on the front and back. Absolutely nothing could be further from the truth. In fact, there are vast numbers of people out there holding down excellent jobs who, at one point in their lives, were made redundant. I was. (OK, it was a long time ago, but I never allowed it to become a burden. And it wasn't.)

Ultimately, your CV will probably show this unexplained 'gap' but, again, the jobs market being what it is, the reason for it is much more common than you might think. My advice for handling the situation at interview is always to 'front up', be honest and say that conditions had become difficult for your previous employer such that your position was forced into redundancy. Potential employers are much more likely to mentally applaud your honesty and if, by that time, they're warming to you anyway, its whole significance is likely to diminish.

The point of this short chapter is to show that redundancy, unwelcome and unexpected as it may be, is definitely *not* the end of the road that some perceive it to be – and may even be the launch-pad for a fantastic new career.

Chapter 3

The Jobs Carousel

A surprising statistic: People in the UK will change jobs, on average, every five years throughout their working life (Public Survey Data 2018). Indeed, more recent surveys suggest that younger workers aren't motivated by the same factors as previous generations, such as a 'job for life', but instead value a good work-life balance and a sense of purpose beyond financial success. 'Millennials' change jobs on average once every 2-3 years and some will actually have four completely different *careers* throughout their lifetime. But then changing your job is not the same thing as changing your career – that's altogether a much greater move and one that requires you to consider a further range of possible options, starting with:

'Why do you want to do it?'. You'll need to carry out some serious research and face up to a number of important questions before you can be sure you're making the right move. The thought of changing jobs or even career will occur to almost everyone at some point in their life. But changing your career is quite a bold step and definitely not one to be taken lightly. Some are happy just to change jobs – within their given sector. In any event, you should first ask yourself three questions: 'Why?' 'What?' 'How?'

Why?

There will always be the 'greener grass syndrome' which, as we all know, is more likely to be illusory anyway. However, there could be any number of legitimate reasons for your wish to make this move, some of which we covered in Chapter 1: the unfulfilled promises made at the initial interview and the possibilities for personal advancement apparently nullified; a consistently low salary; not having your ('superhuman') efforts and achievements appreciated by colleagues or, crucially, your boss; lack of consequently sympathetic communication from above; ... etc, etc. Still, before you rush to write your Pulitzer-esque letter of resignation, it would do no harm to find out whether a move to another department within the organisation or office location might also be possible – and, in fact, the real answer. Of course, this assumes that your 'organisation' is large enough to be able to offer these options, and again, be wary of that green grass...

You may simply wish to get ahead with your career and, if relevant, you should know *why* you want to move sectors entirely. On the other hand, it could be a move from, say, the public to the private sector (or vice versa). If one of the first questions at your interview is (and it probably would be): 'So tell me, Sarah, why do you want to make this move?' you'll need to know the answer – honest and forthright. If you do, excellent. However, if you're seen to be wavering...!

Never denigrate your current or most recent employer, as it will mark you out as 'potential trouble'. Instead, keep it positive by saying, for example, how much you'd learned by being there and felt the need to use these skills in a wider sphere.

What?

What do you really want to do? For example, are you looking to work at home more? Or less? Perhaps you want to be more goal-focused. Would you like a job that involves more travel (local, UK-wide or international)? You may have decided that you want to forge a new career in sales or marketing. Or simply to find something that's more stress-free. People are often put off the idea of making such a move because of their self-perceived 'inadequacies' ('Fly a plane? Me?') but a little research can reveal this not to be the case and, with a bit of application, quite attainable.

These are just examples – the list of new opportunities you can consider is endless – but they all require you to have researched fully the pros and cons of the one you choose. You must be able to identify the pitfalls, or possibly even the need for a further qualification whilst simultaneously appreciating your genuine chances of success. If you see this change of job or career as the next, but final, step, that's fine. However, if it's to be a single step on your path to overall career success and fulfilment, then you must know what this role is all about, what it could possibly offer to you in terms of *genuine* prospects for personal (and financial) advancement and what part it will play in your journey.

How?

OK, you've decided where you want to go. So how are you going to make the move? I've shown already how research is so important in any of these plans, but so is *networking* (see Chapter 6).

If you do want to move to, say, marketing, piloting, the private sector, or the Leeds office, then you could try to speak to and even meet people who are already there. (NB: Be aware that some *may* see this as a threat to their own position and they would probably regard any potential 'interlopers' with suspicion. So tread carefully.) However, you don't need to know them personally, but make contact – and tell them you'd really appreciate their advice (people tend to react well to that). And they, crucially, will probably introduce you to more key people – and on you go...

So how? Use social media: LinkedIn (see Chapter 13) can be an amazing source of people who you will find by inserting the relevant search criteria, e.g., the organization itself; 'sales and marketing' within 'FinTech' in 'Leeds' revealing people who'd probably be delighted to help you. And if you plan to move within your current organisation, the same rule applies. Network.

Of course, alerting colleagues within your own organisation to your plans is possibly full of bear traps as well so be careful and prepared to identify and counter any unwelcome gossip by identifying it as... 'office gossip'. Still, it could actually work in your favour. What you discover through your own networking could change your approach and either help your application enormously – or put you off the idea altogether. A *career* change is, by definition, one step beyond simply a change of job. Nonetheless the same rules of research and networking should apply equally to both.

I have no wish to blur the lines between job change and career change, but the differences can be both subtle and significant. You must choose the path that suits you best.

Ask yourself why you want to move, and whether other options are open to you. Know what this new role entails, whether you're actually capable of doing it, or if further training is required. And, finally, decide how you're going to get in front of the right people, either as part of your research or, indeed, for interview.

Key Points:

- Why move at all?

- Carry out full research.

- What, exactly, is this new role all about?

- Network and, wherever possible, arrange to meet contacts face-to-face.

Chapter 4

Effective Communication

The message here is simplicity itself. Although this book may be seen as being aimed more directly at job-seekers, the ability to communicate simply and effectively applies to *any* approach you might be making to, say, a prospective client or new contact. Strong communication skills are key and, yes, I abide by two distinct beliefs: 'KISS' or, 'Keep it Simple, Stupid' and the fact that 'People employ *People.*' Or 'People buy from people'. (It also helps enormously that they like you – it stands to reason – particularly if they'll be working alongside you.) No-one is going to employ a candidate based on their CV alone or even a letter; but there is a natural process – my 'Three Levels of Communication':

1. A well-written letter or CV can often create the initial interest...

2. A follow-up phone call can enhance that CV through the reader's ability now to hear your (discernible and acceptable) voice...

3. The face-to-face meeting with the reader – the ultimate scenario.

Reaching 'Level 3' is critical. For example, you'd be unlikely to buy a car based purely on what you'd read in the sales brochure. An employer can now engage fully with the individual and see, precisely, what's on offer – how this product might fully meet their needs. This could be your ability to engage easily with their client base, their own team, or both while giving *you* the opportunity to discuss how your 'features & benefits' might actually meet these requirements. Similarly, you, as a candidate, can scrutinize them.

Management:

One of the key qualities of a good manager is that they communicate constantly with their team: What are the principal objectives of this company or department? Where are we placed in relation to the best offerings of our principal competitors, and can we emulate or outdo them? How often do we sit down to communicate ideas between us? Daily? Weekly? Once a month? These managers' attributes demonstrate the sort of so-called 'soft' skills that are much sought after by senior management. Why? Well of course there are myriad management tools available at all levels. However, and back to the benefits of simplicity, any team being led by such an individual will almost certainly out-perform its peer groups.

Inclusive communication really is a crucial element of good management style and if you have it, make sure it's recognized by others.

Chapter 5
How to Approach the Jobs Market

There is a saying, no doubt coined by some grizzled old marketer: "In marketing, if you're trying to talk to everybody, you're not reaching anybody." Mm. As you approach the jobs market, it's probably worth bearing that in mind. Because what you're embarking upon is, in effect, a marketing exercise but with *you* as the product to be marketed, or, ultimately, 'sold'. Many of the techniques involved in marketing can apply here and help to put you in front of your target business(es). However, having first targeted your audience, what you then say to them is crucial – so don't muck it up by talking exclusively about yourself!

When looking for a new job, or even just a change of direction, many people make the same basic mistake: in their desperation to jump on their figurative soap-box and explain, loudly, what they have to offer a waiting public, they fail totally to view themselves through the eyes of the potential employer: 'You see, this is really all about my amazing career and some astounding personal achievements...' – which, quite frankly, is the last thing the employer wants to hear or read about.

Why? Because they are the buyer and you have to imagine yourself as the product that you hope is going to *make their day*; a product that they may well want to buy. So yes, it is a marketing exercise and should be treated as such.

The CV, then, becomes this product's brochure. (See Chapter 7: *Your CV*). And, as with any brochure, it should be both attractive and instantly readable. Employers are often attracted to 'experts' – people who can offer a first-class, recognisable skill or experience that fits well with their own operation and requirements. If, however, your research has shown, or the job description specifically asks for, '...a need for leadership or management skills', or 'sales experience' for example, then simply highlighting the fact that you have such experience is probably not enough. You should be able to provide solid examples specifying exactly where your own experience matches their needs. (See the sample cover letter in Chapter 8.) They need to see whatever 'features and benefits' this product can offer that are likely to attract them the most.

What to say, and how to come across? Your target businesses are probably targets for a reason: you like what they do, how they do it and yes, you'd like to work for them. You must also be prepared to say exactly that to the person you meet there. Remember that people employ people and if you can impress upon them not only your enthusiasm, but also what you can do personally to help their cause, you'll definitely rise in their estimation.

Chapter 6
The Power of Networking

I make no apologies for using 'Power' in this title because its effect can be huge. However, I also have some very simple philosophies when it comes to networking – and how to do so effectively. The key is to have an objective, no matter what that is, and have networking as your means to that end. And the sooner you can convey that objective to your target, the better. Networking 'events' are increasingly abundant and I have a list of noteworthy points about them, including:

- Networking events are useful, but the smaller ones are always better.

- Never be afraid just to smile and introduce yourself; the other person expects it.

- Be calm (even if your nerves are doing quite the opposite).

- Make sure you keep their business card or contact details if you plan to keep in touch. (So many people miss this opportunity, to their great regret...)

- If you decide that you would like either to keep in touch or meet them separately at a later date, suggest you would love to arrange a coffee some time.

- Do not expect instant results. Networking is more likely to be a slow-burn exercise.

Of course there are many people to whom the very thought of 'Networking!' – which they see as little more than unsolicited approaches to strangers, or even friends – initially makes them very uncomfortable.

OK, that's quite understandable. Not everyone has that gregarious streak and, besides, they simply prefer to keep their own counsel. However, they could be missing a host of opportunities which may otherwise never come their way and I do say "initially" uncomfortable because, having tentatively dipped their toe into these uncharted waters, they'll more often than not find networking to be a surprisingly easy medium and very much to their liking and benefit.

As a rule people will try to help other people when they can. That's just a simple fact and one you should be able to capitalise on. They may even suggest a follow-up meeting, which should be seen as encouraging but this does *not* mean that they or indeed everyone you meet is going to offer you a job immediately; goodness, you've hardly reached that stage yet.

But they'll usually be happy to offer advice and ideas, sometimes in areas you hadn't even thought about. And, as I've said, simply asking someone for their advice and/or guidance – rather than for a possible job opportunity – is more likely to have them open their door to you. Why not? They have absolutely nothing to lose – and possibly much to gain.

If there's nothing they can offer directly themselves, they may suggest someone else who they think could be interested in you. Even better, they may actually introduce you to that individual who could, in turn, suggest or introduce you to someone else... and so on. (And meeting someone new but with the endorsement of, e.g., their own colleague or business acquaintance, can be another great advantage.)

Anyway, at each stage of the networking process, you're making a mark, creating a memorable 'personality' in their eyes which simply would not exist if all they had was a CV or cover letter. Indeed, as we know, the sole purpose of those two should remain to get you in front of the reader in the first place – and so the networking begins.

Preparation:

Do prepare for a face-to-face chat with someone. You have initially to 'deliver the first serve', as it were, to justify fairly quickly your credentials and your reason for suggesting the meeting.

The opportunities that this ground-breaking meeting now produces can be endless:

- you may be seen as an (unexpectedly) perfect fit for a role they have in mind

- you may be further introduced to someone who thinks the same thing: 'I think you should meet our Operations Manager. I believe he could be very interested…'

- they may come back to you weeks, or even months, later with a new proposal because, having met you, they were impressed enough to do so (and this often happens)

- they may even suggest an alternative, but perfectly viable, option or role that you would never have considered by yourself. Wow!

Put simply, the more people who have actually met you and are able to 'archive' you in their bank of contacts, the greater the chance that they'll recall you when, later, they're looking for someone with your skillset. Or they know someone who is. Abiding by the "People employ people" principle – and if people know that you're 'on the radar', so to speak, they may now start talking about you to their own contacts, colleagues, friends... then further meetings will follow. And you should never refuse a meeting; with *anyone*. You simply don't know who might turn up, what will be discussed or where it might lead. You could be pleasantly surprised.

Finally, your own close network is bound to be much larger than you think. If you write the names of everyone you know, there will be "... oh yes, of course...!" moments and these could prove to be a source who will lead you, immediately or over time, to a hugely effective contact. LinkedIn[1] can also be extremely useful and it enables you to

---

[1] See Chapter 13: LinkedIn

trawl for known contacts; and then make contact with them...

It's in our nature to communicate with others and networking is vital to our success. Don't be disheartened if it doesn't bear fruit immediately. Persevere, because in the end it most certainly will.

Christmas Networking – a great opportunity that's often missed:

As Christmas approaches, major boardroom decisions tend to become fewer, as their outcomes are unlikely to be introduced before well into the new year anyway.

But although I agree that things are likely to quieten down at this time of year, it's also worth bearing in mind that, between Christmas and New Year, CEOs or even 'senior director types' will want to escape the bedlam that their happy home has become and possibly seek solace in the office – where they'll arrive wearing jeans & trainers (surprising the skeleton staff), brew their own coffee, stick their feet up on the desk – figuratively speaking – and be free to chat liberally with, say, *you*. I see it as a fantastic window of opportunity that's often open, but rarely exploited. The point is that, after New Year, it's almost certainly closed again.

Chats of this sort can be extremely beneficial for both parties as they can be carried out in a sort of quasi-informal and relaxed manner – where they can ask the sort of questions unlikely to be asked at a formal interview and so find out about the *real* you – as, indeed, can you about them. And don't be put off by their apparent inaccessibility. Try phoning their office directly (OK, even better if you do have their mobile number...), failing which email; text; whatever. If you're in another country, suggest a Zoom call at a mutually convenient time. I see this as a tried and tested method and, generally speaking, the key person will applaud your inventiveness – if not your cheek. But then "Faint heart never won fair lady."

Chapter 7

Your CV

How do you write a CV? When it comes down to it, most people simply haven't a clue where to start. Of course, they can list the various jobs they've had; but then, in an apparent need to include absolutely every aspect of their career to date – 'just in case' – the final result will then be, invariably, far too long and with much of the relevant information totally obscured by the glaringly irrelevant. Remember, your CV should be a *brochure* for a product. And that product is You; therefore, it should be a marketing document designed purely with the reader in mind.

Your CV Profile (i.e., the first thing they'll read) should follow these same rules, again keeping in mind your target audience. Wherever possible, decide what market sector might benefit from your own skillset and appeal to it. (It can also be quite effective to use a brief extract from a personal reference or LinkedIn recommendation, thus offering an independent endorsement of your claims.) Your profile should appeal immediately to the reader. To illustrate, picture this: You meet someone new:

'What do you do?' she asks.

'I'm an architect,' you say.

'Oh, really?' she answers. 'Have you designed any buildings I've seen?'

'Possibly,' you reply. 'We did the new student centre at the university...'

'Oh wow,' she says. 'That's a beautiful building...'

Without trying – and without blowing your own trumpet (note 'we' did the new student centre...), you've made a great impression. Now picture *this*, you again meet someone new:

'What do you do?' he asks.

'Well, I'm a passionate, innovative, dynamic provider of architectural services with a collaborative approach to creating and delivering an outstanding, world-class user experience.' (!)

Mm. OK... Great. You may think that second example is probably a bit over the top, but it's a quote taken directly from a CV and yes, I used to see them all the time. The example below makes the common mistake of using pointless hyperbole in the profile: ('extremely' value-driven; 'passionately' interested) in a vain effort to 'build up' the CV. Nor is it enhanced by having nine 'Key Skills'. Key skills should reflect the fact that they are, in fact, 'key' – i.e., what you are *really* good at and, consequently, a maximum of four (targeted at the specific needs of the reader) is sufficient. The longer the list, the more diluted the 'skills' that are being claimed becomes. And yet the vast majority of CVs seem to have such an extended list, mainly because the writers want to include absolutely everything they've done – no matter how 'key' (or otherwise) they are. Absolutely pointless.

Here is an example:

Joseph Brown

Glasgow, G77 0HA. xyzxyz@gmail.com

07715-xxxxxx

PROFILE:

A highly experienced strategic and operational manager extremely value driven and passionately interested in people and their development. His strengths include: being authentic and collaborative, leading with integrity and working in partnership with his team by being fair and building trust and respect. He is known to motivate others to sign up to and achieve shared goals, with an ability to be diplomatic and stakeholder aware, having both initiated and implemented strategic business plans with excellent results, he constantly provides direction and leadership, especially during times of change.

Determination and a keen eye for service delivery and quality also means that he can quickly assess stakeholder requirements and succeeds by communicating this to others. Commercially astute, he is a strong communicator, with the ability to influence effectively by using excellent presentation, written and oral communication skills.

KEY SKILLS:

- Project Management
- Strategic Planning and Implementation
- Education

- CPD Training
- Mentoring Internal
- External Relationship Building
- Organizational Change Management
- Collaboration
- Knowledge Transfer

(175 words)

However, how about:

Sarah Green
Glasgow, G77 0HA. xyzxyz@gmail.com
07715-xxxxxx

PROFILE:

A highly qualified and experienced strategic operational manager and collaborative leader with a strong background in CRM at senior level. Having played an integral role as a member of a Senior Management Team, her strengths also include building trust and respect while motivating others to achieve shared goals. Diplomatic and stakeholder-aware, she is also quick to support senior management, having personally both initiated and implemented strategic business plans with excellent results.

(Sarah was an extremely hard worker who constantly motivated her team to produce great results. She became personally responsible for a 35% uplift in her section's profitable turnover. I recommend her without hesitation.)
- [Charles Smith – CEO, Bloggs & Co.]

KEY SKILLS:

- Strong leadership and motivational skills
- Project Management
- Strategic Planning for Change
- Leadership

(128 words)

The first of these two CV examples was followed by seven further pages of 'experience', little of which would have been of any interest to the reader. We managed to reduce that to two-and-a-half pages. The CV Profile should summarise the skills and relevant experience of the writer and in fact, she'd managed to do that superbly in her closing sentence: "Commercially astute, she is a strong communicator with the ability to influence effectively, using excellent presentation, written and oral communication skills." *Six relevant* skills wrapped in a short sentence, from which the reader can mentally upload the information easily.

Like any good brochure (for a car, a holiday or a wood-burning stove), your CV should immediately grab the reader's attention. This is, we hope, a 'warm' market. They are the (interested) customer and as any successful salesman or marketer will tell you, you need first to know a) what does the customer really need or want? and b) what can you offer them that will meet these needs? Simple, no? But anything else, which may be of great interest to you but bear no relevance whatsoever to them or their organisation, should be either deleted or minimised in importance.

Think about their true requirements, examine every statement or achievement claim you're making and ask yourself: "So what?" It may be relevant to you – but not to them and, if so, it's only taking up valuable space and possibly even distracting them from the key issues. If you really do think that it's actually a key point worth airing, do so when you meet them at interview (or first meeting) when you have their 100% attention. Think: 'If in doubt, take it out.' Adopting this level of simplicity applies equally to a general CV (aka 'My CV') and so it becomes much easier to edit in the case of a specific approach.

Nobody wants to wade through pages of verbiage while trying to decipher what's being said or claimed, certainly not busy people (who probably have a pile of other CVs to consider anyway). In most cases, it's better to be too short than too long. Because if you've already established your credibility, they may well be keen to see more of it at an interview. However, surprising as it may seem, they'll want simply to be able to pick it up and apply the 'three Ws':

- What have they done?
- With whom?
- Where do their key skills lie?

If, while scanning the first page, they can mentally apply ticks to those three Ws, an interview will probably follow – if only to satisfy their curiosity: 'Mm. Interesting. I wonder if...' Remember that the CV has that one single purpose: to get you an interview, or at least a meeting with the reader. Just as with a sales brochure, the more easily they can see just how attractive and potentially beneficial this product is, the more likely they'll be to want to see it in person. Think like them.

It's essential to keep your CV such that even an 11-year-old child could easily read, understand and repeat what's written. No-one expects your CV to be a work of literary genius – although spelling or grammatical errors will always be a total turn-off. All the reader really needs to know are the bare facts in order to decide if they want to meet you. Or not. Think of the 'Three Ws'. And if you've managed to cover them anyway, then the CV has done its job.

Although not always clear from the advert or job description, it may be that your potential 'target' is really looking for someone whose peripheral skills are equally important. For example, showing a knowledge and experience of, say, basic accounting might increase your chances with someone who's looking for an experienced sales manager – but also with the financial acumen to produce management accounts and read a balance sheet. Get 'behind the lines' and view the role from *their* perspective...

Chapter 8

Your Cover Letter

The cover letter is an extremely important part of the job application process. Just like the CV, it has one job: to make the reader want to meet you. "So how will I impress them enough to have them want to meet me?"

Whether they read the CV, your LinkedIn profile (Chapter 13) or the letter first is almost immaterial, as one should complement the other – both in length and content. However, the principle throughout remains the same: with the letter, keep it simple, focused upon *them* and, above all, enthusiastic. If they've read and liked one, they should also like the other – simply confirming their positive views about you.

If you're sending out multiple applications, there's a tendency to create a standard letter template and all you do is, essentially, change the name of the recipient accordingly. *Big* mistake! Anyone reading it will almost certainly see it as a 'general' letter and will bin it immediately (wouldn't you?). Although much of the body of the letter referring to your experience may well remain the same, you must 'individualise' each letter by referring directly to them, their company or organisation – and their specific needs. Show that you know and understand them and how you can actually be of benefit to them in this (or other, non-specified) role.

Basic Rules

Avoid the trap of being so eager to say just how wonderful you are that you fill vast paragraphs with meaningless words in an attempt to cover all bases. What you will end up with are long, meandering sentences, the meanings of which are often totally lost on the reader (who's rapidly losing interest anyway).

Instead, it should include those three to four principal paragraphs which lay out, simply and directly, why you're enthusiastic and attracted to the role, how your experience not only meets but possibly exceeds their needs and, finally, that you would genuinely welcome the chance to explain all this to them in person.

- **Do not repeat, verbatim, phrases from the job advert.** By all means refer to them but simply to show that you understand the requirement and can offer that sort of experience.

- ***Do* show enthusiasm;** people like enthusiasts. This can be for the company / organisation; or the role; or both. But it must come across as genuine and sincere.

- **Do not 'justify' the text.** On a letter, aligning left is correct.

So many cover letters fail due to a lack of preparation and care. Just like the CV, they offer a vital window on you and rarely will someone who wrote a poor or mediocre letter make it to interview. Of all the letters they read, yours must really stand out if you're to have any chance at all. You cannot trust simply to good fortune...

A sample letter:

123 High Street,
Anytown,
AB21 2CD
07710-123456; SmithJane123@gmail.com

Yvonne McAllister,
HR Manager,
HALO Trust,
LONDON, SW1 4DS.
25th December, 2022

Dear Ms McAllister,

International Operations Staff - HALO:

I am writing in response to your advertisement for the above and would like very much to be considered for the role.

HALO offers me the perfect opportunity not only to use my skills and experience to great effect but your job description also summarises exactly the sort of role in which I believe I would flourish; more important to this, it's where I could make a positive contribution.

The relevant experience I offer combines the exceptional skills - including leadership - refined by my time in the army as a junior officer, with the experience gained while with the NHS and Macmillan Trust where I also developed the ability to communicate effectively with those who, through illness or disability, find communication difficult.

During my career I have been required to show a large degree of determination and compassion, both traits which I would be able to bring to the various requirements and challenges of this role. Very happy working in a team environment, nonetheless I have also proved that I can rise to a challenge, both in work and the sporting arena.

I cannot emphasise enough my genuine interest in this role and I hope very much to be able to discuss it with you in more detail.

Yours sincerely,
Jane Smith

Chapter 9

The 'Hidden Market' and how to make a Speculative Approach

Your primary objective is to meet the right people. And the 'right people' may not necessarily be the individuals who, ultimately, offer you a job. Yet they are the ones who will, almost certainly, play a significant part in that process so that the initial meeting can often be a starting point for a sequence of events that could well result in an offer (job or sales) being made.

In order to be able to speak to your target businesses, you must first establish why on earth they might want to speak to you! Put yourself in their shoes: would you respond positively to a speculative approach from someone who just contacted you randomly – out of *hope*? Almost certainly not. So, you must a) do your research, b) think like they think and c) show how your key knowledge, skills and experience will benefit them – rather than you.

It's been said that the so-called 'Hidden Market' comprises 'between 70% and 80% of the current vacancies that remain unadvertised'. Really? Hmm.

However, the Hidden Market does exist and these positions often fall into one of four different categories. If there's a genuine vacancy about which employers are fully aware, there are different options open to them before they have to resort to advertising. For example, they could:

- Attempt to fill it internally

- Poach from a competitor

- Employ a professional recruiter/head-hunter

- Quietly 'put the word about' – and await results. (More common with senior roles.)

The fact is, there's a definite requirement here and so an obvious opportunity for you to secure a speculative meeting – even in the first three situations, where there is no certainty of their filling the post immediately. And if they *are* using a recruiter, they could also benefit by employing you directly and saving themselves a substantial fee.

Much more important, however, is that there are times when a vacancy exists 'in principle' but it hasn't yet reached the stage where an organised search has started. For example, during senior management meetings, there can often be said: 'What we need, I suppose, is a...' In other words, there's a need for someone to come in and fill that role effectively and they're all aware of it, but the post has not actually been fully defined yet. A well-timed approach by you could work extremely well in your favour.

And then there are situations where no position actually exists – at least in the minds of senior management – but which could well be created by your pointing out where there's a gap in their armoury. Again, this may simply be because of current circumstances (e.g., expanding [or declining] markets, fierce competition, takeovers, mergers) and there's an opportunity to be exploited. You need to:

a) identify that opportunity and

b) present yourself as a possible solution.

But then how do you find and identify these opportunities?

The internet is alive with recruiting activity and even the recruitment pages of the daily newspapers still carry advertised vacancies (once or twice a week). But the main national newspapers – not just the FT – have 'Business' sections every day. And so, every day there are stories about companies and their various activities, possibly involving expansion or even changes in company policy and it pays to search through these for the opportunities they present; their requirements may well fit you exactly.

Similarly, there are many trade publications, professional magazines and even website news pages which will offer 'Careers' sections as well as stories about business activities that may also be relevant to you and your experience. This is where it's essential to strike fast and a well worded letter, mentioning the specific article and showing your interest could really impress them and, consequently, lead to a useful discussion. If you leave it too late, time will have moved on and the immediate impact will have been lost. If possible, you want to avoid referring to: '... the article in last Tuesday's FT'.

Before you make any approach, however, you must be sure that you can present yourself (or your ideas) in a way that will, at the very least, arouse their interest. What are you going immediately to *sell* them? What, exactly, is this product or idea that's going to attract them enough to make them agree to a meeting? Are they even going to be interested in someone like you?

Again, wherever possible, you must put yourself in their position and determine in your own mind what the key component is. At this stage, however, you certainly want to avoid any suggestion that you're looking for a job (unless that subject has been agreed already) and so a 'soft' approach is essential. You might propose a brief discussion on ways in which you see their business going and an idea that you have which may help it to progress. One would hope that they would at least be intrigued enough to want to know more.

A well-aimed search through relevant websites can provide masses of information about companies, agencies, public bodies, professional firms and organisations. As well as (possibly) offering contact information, they will often mention their new markets, expertise and areas of speciality which can provide a useful hook onto which you can hang your prime reason contacting them in the first place.

Once you've succeeded in gaining an initial, 'informal' meeting, you must prepare for it with the same attention to detail that you would for a full interview. People will respond much more readily to someone who has clearly prepared and knows not only what they're talking about, but enough about the target company, its people, its markets, its clients – to be impressive.

Remember – this is simply a first stage on the road to obtaining an offer. The very fact that you can talk about a company or organisation gives you a much greater chance to promote yourself to the next stage. This could be a subsequent meeting with colleagues ("... I'd like you to meet our Sales Director/other members of the management team...") or simply another opportunity to air your ideas. But the initial step has been taken and that's the most important one.

Here's a sample extract from speculative letter of a sort you do *not* want to write:

> Dear Sir,
>
> I am writing to you because, having recently been made redudant from my previous role at Bloggs & Co, I believe that your company would benefit from my particular skills and experience...

Whereas it's unlikely that anyone would write something quite as crass as this, many writers do fall into the same trap: It's all about 'Me, me, me...' However, at this stage, there's really only one person interested in you: You. There's a need, therefore, to create that same interest within the reader.

As ever, put yourself in their shoes: what's going to make them sit up and say, 'Mm, now this is interesting.'? Reading about themselves, their company or organisation, a reference to specific issues that they might be facing or plans they're contemplating – and how you might help them to address these issues – is far more interesting to them than a monologue about... you. Why? Because it shows you care. Oh yes. If, however, your letter does none of these things and it's fairly obvious that this is simply a standard approach, looking for something from them, unfocused and with 'Dear Sir' or even 'Dear Sir/Madam' tacked on to the top, then its next port of call is likely to be the bin; and quite right too.

Again, this letter has that same job: to make the reader want to meet you. The principles for the letter remain: keep it brief, simple and, above all, *enthusiastic.*

A good opening sentence should always refer to the target organisation and, if possible, a direct reference to the recipient and/or the issue(s) at hand. By immediately engaging them like this, you have established a connection which at least shows that this letter is meant for them alone and not some wide trawl.

> Dear Mr Jones,
>
> During a recent visit to your Wetherfield site for the SMAS event, I was struck by two things: the site facilities - and your evident focus on developing people. This interested me a great deal as these values closely align with my own, for example...

A large number of cover or speculative letters fail to reach their target due to a lack of preparation and care. Remember, only rarely will someone who wrote a poor or mediocre letter make it to interview. Yours has really to stand out if you are to have any chance at all. You cannot trust simply to good fortune. So, remember:

- It's not about you – it's about *them.*

- Carry out extensive research (half-hearted is no good at all).

- Check out websites, media and existing employees.

- Identify your key (relevant and attractive) skills.

- Edit your CV (the 'brochure') accordingly.

Chapter 10

'Follow up' suggestions...

This chapter covers the increasingly ancient art of the telephone call and how to use it to your advantage. With the advent of electronic communication, of course it's less common these days. Nonetheless, whereas it may indeed be a dying art, your skill in using it can still pay dividends and, if you can achieve it, this call directly to your 'target' individual can be extremely useful – for both of you.

Having written your speculative letter, waited for the appropriate number of days – and assuming they haven't called you back immediately to arrange a meeting – you will now want to follow up with a phone call. To some people this is second nature – particularly those with a sales and marketing background – but many will undoubtedly find the prospect daunting, inducing levels of stress normally associated with a first interview! But treat people with honesty and courtesy and they will, almost always, react positively.

Of course, as ever, the one thing you want to achieve is that all-important meeting. Nothing else counts. So, you really do need to look at the situation through the eyes of the person you're about to contact: the 'Target'. Clearly, you want to speak to them but often you'll first have to deal with a senior receptionist or personal (often 'executive' assistant these days). And although there are some who definitely take this aspect of their job very seriously, most are doing nothing more than protecting their boss from what they see as unsolicited and unnecessarily time-wasting calls – often many times a day. It's always a good start, therefore, to acknowledge this fact and perhaps to take the edge off any resistance by suggesting that they might be the one to speak to at this stage:

'Hello. My name is Joe Bloggs. You may recall I wrote to Laura Smith last week, and I'm really just following up on that. Now I do know that you're probably very busy, but I assume that you also look after Laura's diary? I wonder, do you think it would be possible to find a space for a very brief chat with her next week?'

You've acknowledged their position and graciously handed the decision-making to them. They're now much more likely to respond positively – mainly because you've shown a courtesy often missed by others. However, you don't want to appear too obsequious as they may simply dismiss you out of hand. But the chances are that they will, for now at least, show the same courtesy to you as a result, and you must still be aware of the sort of things they might say – and then how to counter!

It may be that you're put straight through to your 'Target', in which case you must be able to exhibit the same control and warmth of spirit simultaneously. Remember, this is purely a speculative approach and, for now, you only want her to agree to a meeting – however brief. You must be able to suggest that this will be a positive idea – for you both. So, as a slight variation on the above:

> *'Hello, Ms Smith, thanks for taking my call. You'll realise I'm really following up on my letter and, as I mentioned there to Angela (you should have got Angela's name by now.), I was wondering if it might be possible to arrange a brief chat. I do appreciate you're busy but I also believe it could be useful. Do you have a space in your diary during the next week?'*

Not a heavy-handed approach and the essence here is: 'In – Strike – Out'. This is not the time to get involved in the detail, even if she wants to. Your message is always going to be delivered best by you in person, so don't allow her to extend the discussion at this point:

> *'It probably would be better if I were to explain things to you fully when we meet. So, Thursday at 3 o'clock? Yes, thank you, I look forward to seeing you then.'*

But in order to get to this happy stage, you may have to clamber over a few obstacles. It's easy to be deflected but, just as with salary negotiation, it's imperative that you keep the initiative.

Below is a selection of 10 typical openings, both from the EA/PA (we'll call them EA for now) and your intended target – and suggested responses which should allow you to keep the initiative, without being 'pushy':

1. EA says: 'Target is not available':

> *'Yes, I thought she might be busy. But you can probably help me here; when do you think it would be a good time to call back?'*

2. EA says: 'Target will phone you back'. (You've potentially lost the initiative.):

> *'Thanks very much. But look, I'm actually going to be in and out of meetings/away from*

a phone most of today. Perhaps I could call back later? But I'll need your help here: when do you think she might be free?' (You've kept the initiative.)

3. EA says: 'Target isn't interested in speaking to you...' Don't just take it on the chin: 'Oh, OK then. Goodbye.' If you do, you're gone. Better at least to try:

'Oh, I'm sorry to hear that. I wonder, did she say why?'

It keeps the door ajar and allows you to follow up again. If it's appropriate, you might say:

'Ah, I see. I quite understand, but tell me, is there anyone else in the company who you think I should approach?'

4. EA says: 'Send your CV.'

'Thanks, Angela. Shall I send it to you, or directly to Ms Smith? Would it be OK if I call back in a few days?'

5. Target says: 'Send your CV, and I'll get back to you.'

'Right – I'll send it today. I'm going to be difficult to get hold of over the next couple of days; would it be alright if I called you back on, say, Friday?'

6. Target says: 'OK, but why, exactly, do you want to meet me?'

'Well because I know that I can only explain my ideas to you properly face-to-face – and also I believe that you would gain more from it than by merely discussing it on the phone.' (You may think that's a bit cheesy, but you'd be surprised by how well it works.)

7. Target says: 'There's really no point in further discussion'.

"I see, and I'm sorry to have bothered you. Perhaps I could ask your advice, though: If you were me, where would you be targeting this sort of idea. In fact, do you have any thoughts about who I might contact?"

You never know... and she may be feeling charitable... (Ditto)

8. Target says that she will pass my CV to the HR Director:

'OK, thanks very much. Tell me, would it be OK with you if I were to give him a call in a day or two? Good. I take it I can say that you and I have already spoken?'

9. Target suggests meeting the next time she is in my area:

'Well, that sounds great. Do you have any idea when that might be? Right, I'll put a note in my diary'. When that time comes around, and if you're still waiting to hear, you can always call/text her again: 'Hi, I'm sorry to be chasing you but I was just checking my diary – do you still want to arrange that meeting?'

10. Target says: 'You're just looking for a job, aren't you"?

'Well, no, I really was just hoping for a meeting at this stage. It would be up to you to decide whether anything further comes of it, but your advice would be useful; it rather depends on what we discuss.'

(These are simply ideas to help you with possible responses and not everyone will work; clearly, you'll have to use your own words. Much will depend on the person at the other end of the phone, but after a few calls, you'll soon find that most of it will come naturally.)

Chapter 11

OK, so what exactly are my key skills?

Our British tendency towards modesty can often make the identification, and subsequent presentation, of our own skills quite difficult. But we need not only to be able to identify skills we might possess, but also to know how or why they could appeal to someone else.

In some ways, modesty can be seen as an endearing quality. Indeed, it's a very human trait but which, sadly, can often lead to great opportunities being missed.

It's so important to be able to identify your own skills, particularly those that might be useful to an employer. Because when you approach someone in the hope of being offered a job, as we've said, you're essentially presenting yourself as a product – with its attendant features and benefits – and the employer as the customer. That, simply, is the process here.

For example, whenever we buy anything, from a dishwasher to a car, we've considered closely the various features as the possible benefits that might apply to us and, subsequently, make a decision to buy based on these facts. So, when we consider our own features, we're able to present them as skills. Knowing what these skills are, and why they might appeal to the 'customer' – or potential employer – is vital.

To identify these in ourselves we should discard, for a moment, any natural modesty we might have. Then we can examine our own work history in detail, year by year if necessary, assessing our achievements – however small – and what skills we used at that time. We might be surprised to discover that we can claim more by way of skills than we thought.

Of course, some skills are easy to identify, such as those employed by a tailor or a surgeon, but some less so. The so-called 'soft' skills, for example those often employed by a good manager and which can include motivation, leadership, communication or a great capacity for persuading people, are just as important – as anyone involved in sales will tell you.

A good way of identifying the skills we have already is to review our CV and place on the front page just four key skills that we know we can do in our sleep and which will appeal to the reader, whoever they may be. We now know that a long list of 'skills' – or mainly attributes – on a CV is pointless as it's really seen as just that: a long list. The longer the list, the more dilute each 'skill' becomes. (See Chapter 7: Your CV)

Generally speaking, most people can offer a range of specific skills, e.g., the ability to ride well or to cook a stunning meal, while also being able to audit a set of business accounts. However, only one of those skills is likely to appeal to a prospective employer. We need to be selective, do our research and really know what our attraction is and how then to capitalise on it.

Finally, we should be able to distinguish between a 'skill' and an 'attribute'. Very simply, a skill is something that can be gained through experience and/or tuition. In most cases, however, an attribute tends to be something we were born with. It's often a very fine distinction – and easily confused.

Our own personal skills are extremely important – both to us and a potential employer – and the ability to identify these and see them as potential benefits in what is the 'product' (ourself) is vital in our being able to present a brand image. Once we have a range of known skills from which to draw, we can work with those individually to great effect.

Chapter 12

The Interview
(exploding some myths)

(This chapter addresses the aspects and issues that surround a standard job interview, as opposed to a 'meeting' generated by you. However, many of these are identical anyway and so should be read as such.)

Having reached the stage where a prospective employer wants to meet you, you're at least taking the first real steps towards a job offer. Your CV and cover letter have done their job and, whereas you might face stiff competition, at least you now have the chance to present your case in person. One thing is certain: you must demonstrate an overwhelming sense of enthusiasm for the position; anything less and, quite frankly, you may as well stay at home.

However, an interview should, ideally, be a meeting of minds – an 'inter-view'. It's been estimated that as many as 30% of interviews fail because of issues with the interviewer – *not* the interviewee. In fact, the ideal scenario would be simply a face-to-face conversation or chat between you and the interviewer, an idea that's being increasingly embraced by 'young' companies. (And how forward-looking is *that*?) But the ability to engage with one another is crucial and it really is just as much the job of the interviewer to sell their product as it is for you to sell yours. They should not, therefore, turn it into a form of inquisition as there is rarely much to be gained there by either party. But, sadly, it's not always the case – and you should be prepared.

Preparation, preparation, preparation:

Obviously, visit their website; but explore the site *fully*. Find out all there is to know as it may give details on your team, their work, achievements, recent deals. Visit the News page (but do check the date of the news article...) What have they been doing recently that may be relevant to you, or the team you're hoping to join? Or is there something to talk about to show your interest in them? A question I often ask during mock interviews is: "Tell me, John, what did you think about our website?" For both parties, this is a great question. It allows them to establish the level of your research for the role while also, with luck, gaining a free review of their website. For you, it enables you to express your views on the site, purely from a reader's perspective. Does it 'fill in all the blanks' and truly inform the reader about the principal function, strengths and aims of the business? The floor, at that point, is totally yours.

If you have contacts who work within the organisation then, contacted discreetly, these can be a useful source of inside information.

Reconnaissance:

Assuming this is not to be a remote or 'Zoom' meeting, make absolutely certain you know where the interview is to be held. If you can, visit it the day before. You may be wrong: what you *thought* was Buchanan Street is actually Buchanan *Avenue* or (at worst) your interview is in another part of town completely! If possible, try to do a 'dry run' by visiting the site before-hand. You'll then be aware of issues such as massive and unavoidable roadworks. Go into the building. Meet the receptionist and say you're checking it out '... prior to an interview here tomorrow morning.' When you arrive the next day, the chances are that the first face you'll see will be a friendly one. Good move.

Finally, make sure you have a contact name and telephone number in case of a last-minute emergency. If possible, have a direct contact number for the interviewer or HR. It's the sort of thing they'd usually be unwilling to share but if you phrase your question in the correct way, they will probably give it to you. You now have the direct dial number of your interviewer...

On the day of the interview:

Aim to arrive early (10 mins). This not only means you should be there on time but it also allows you a final appearance check before you launch into the meeting.

Now, switch off your mobile (!)

Always be pleasant and courteous to anyone you meet. It'll help to calm any nerves you might have as any non-threatening conversation would. But remember, you're on view from the moment you enter the building until the moment you leave – and, even then, until you're out of sight! You never know who they might ask for a second opinion.

If they then suggest that you walk with them some distance to an interview room, for example, engage them in light conversation if they haven't already done so. This 'guide' may be simply an HR staff member, but their opinion could well be sought – and so will count. An extended silence would not help here and may even be a way of them testing your initiative. Comment on anything: their paintings, impressive building, spaciousness of the surroundings – but keep it positive and relaxed. Do *not* make it sound rehearsed and don't dwell on it. Besides, it's so much better than the usual boring complaints about the weather or traffic, and helps to develop further the positive relationship that will lead to a successful interview.

The Interview itself:

First impressions are vital – and are formed, literally, in milliseconds. Assuming this is the first interview with them, the interviewer will have no alternative than to imagine you in only neutral terms, based on the information they've taken from your CV or LinkedIn[2] and you have a very brief moment during which to *exceed* these expectations. (If you can do that, you'll have started the whole interview process as positively as possible: "Mm... Like this one.") Good eye contact, smile, firm (dry!) handshake and a relaxed, confident manner are all essential. Without being ridiculously OTT, show them that you're really looking forward to this meeting.

---

[2] If your LinkedIn photo is really a true likeness, fine. If it's not, or one taken 20 years ago – change it!

Answering questions:

The key purpose of an interview is to establish whether you have the level of experience they need, the ability to engage productively with staff and clients alike as well as the sort of character to make things actually happen. Clearly, an interview for a senior director role will differ from that of, say, a Warehouse Operative as the requirements of the more senior role will be greater than the other. In any interview, however, it helps enormously if you can at least appear to be relaxed and confident of your ability to do this specific job. Avoid a tendency to answer questions in a monosyllabic way because doing so will tell the interviewer nothing about your character and, thereby, how likely you'd be to get along with your peer group or customers.

Many interviews these days are 'competency based'. In brief: if they're looking for, say, an IT Auditor, they might ask, "Give me an example of a problem you faced with an IT security issue – and how did you solve it?", or a common approach is: "Give me an example of how you've dealt with a highly stressful situation in your current job." Obviously, the style and subject matter of the questions will vary depending upon the position, but the more technical ones will require you to show your expert knowledge, an understanding of their requirements and how they fit together.

Much has been written on this subject and a generally recognised way of answering competency-based questions is to use the so-called **SAR** method:

Situation – Action – Result

The **Situation** was this...

The **Action** I/we took to address the problem involved...

The (hugely successful) **Result** was...

What works here is for you to condense these situations into a story – an anecdote even. They can relate to them more easily than to a list of facts, no matter how relevant or (potentially) interesting those facts may be. However, it's important to make these stories both interesting and *memorable*. Then you will be. Adults, like children, do remember stories, especially good ones... And if, during the following weeks, they remember your story, they will also remember you.

Many people are affected by nerves. Quite understandable. However, you must remember that, in the majority of cases, the interviewer wants and encourages you to be good and to offer the best of you. Why? Because they have an outstanding requirement and they really do want *you* to be the one to meet it. Nerves can affect you in different ways and you must be aware of these. For example, you may a) find it difficult to maintain eye contact or b) suffer from 'rabbit in the headlights' syndrome and have a tendency to 'freeze' mid-way through your narrative. Don't worry.

The best way to perform at interview is not to 'perform'. Instead of treating this as some sort of tortuous test, in which you answer quite correctly but in a stiff and formal way, you should try to imagine that you're speaking to a friend or colleague – or to a group of friends. Relax, smile, laugh even. They'll be keen to see how you'd work with their key clients anyway, or how you'd fit within their own team. People react positively to humour and you may want to offer this as an aspect of your own management style, indicating a lightness of touch which most people will appreciate. It's so much more attractive, and once having broken that invisible 'barrier' you'll find it much easier to engage with the interviewer(s); which is actually what they want.

So yes, an interview can be face-to-face with one individual, more than one, or even a panel. You'll tend to be more comfortable when dealing with one person and it's bound to be easier to engage with an individual than with three. However, if there is more than one interviewer, it's *vital* that you include and maintain eye contact with them *all*. Any one of them who is thus left out of the 'magic circle' will be unlikely to favour you when final votes are cast.

There are times when the relevant manager will conduct the interview – a role they will often carry out with poor grace. The whole process of recruiting a new member of staff can be a distraction for busy people – and the less time wasted on unsuitable candidates and fruitless interviews, the better. The more impressive you can be from the start, and then through the interview process itself, the closer they'll be to reaching that goal – and getting back to work. What is important to all interviewers, however, is how you will fit – with them, with other members of the team, and with their clients (both existing and new).

You must create a relationship with the interviewer so that they like you from the start. As well as enthusiasm, people will tend to react well to positive thinking, and someone who can show a clear understanding of how their organisation works. The more information you can gain about a company, its products and aspirations, markets, competition, its people – the list is endless – then, clearly, the more attractive you'll be to them.

Never 'refuse' a job until it's been offered to you.

In an effort to establish a solid position, many people can, inadvertently, make the mistake of introducing provisions and other negative thinking to the discussion. These can put people off. The time to introduce any problems or objections is *after they have offered you the job* – i.e., after they've 'crossed the Rubicon', as I put it, and decided to 'buy'. At that stage, you are the one they want and any issues you may raise will likely be seen as, essentially, unimportant and perfectly 'fixable' in their haste to have you 'signing on the dotted line'.

However, a typical example could unfold thus: The interview is going splendidly – but the role is based in Glasgow. You live in Edinburgh. They ask: "Would this pose any problems for you?" If you say something like, "Well, it's a hellish commute – but I'm sure I'd manage..." you've already introduced a measure of doubt in their minds and your CV now hovers over the 'Mm. Possible' pile.

Better to say, "Absolutely no problem. I was planning to move to Glasgow anyway." If you do get the job and decide instead to commute after all, the chances of them bringing it up with you six months later are extremely remote. Besides, they're very close to achieving their goal and, for now, small details are likely to be brushed aside as being of little importance in their willingness to tie things up with as little fuss as possible: 'So – your own coffee machine? Sure, I think that can be arranged. Can you still start on Monday?'

Your questions:

As the interview draws to a close, you will, almost certainly, be asked if you have any questions for them – which, of course, you will! These must be relevant to them, the position, their future plans, their client base, the previous job-holder (if any?). (Questions about things such as holiday entitlement or their overtime régime should definitely be avoided at this time.) Good advice, however, is to write your questions down, in brief, on a card to act as a reminder which can be produced and referred to at the time. This shows that, not only do you have an organised mind, you've also prepared for the interview and are taking it seriously. It can also help *you* to be reassured that you'll not be caught by a total memory failure when it comes to question time – even if you do have an excellent memory. However, you must avoid asking questions about a topic they've covered already...

The Close:

There's often a danger that, at the point where the interviewer says: "Alright, that just about wraps it up for now. We'll be in touch in the next week or so." or something like that and you deflate like a pricked balloon. The interview's over and your guard comes down. It can cause serious damage to what had been, until then, an excellent performance, and you should beware. Always leave with as much enthusiasm for them and the job as you did throughout the interview:

'Well, thank you very much, Justin/Gloria. From what you've told me, this is precisely what I'm looking for and I really look forward to hearing from you again soon...' at least demonstrates real and genuine enthusiasm both for them and the role; if they like you, it's precisely what they want to hear. Besides, it's so much better than, simply: 'Well, thanks very much. Goodbye.'

You must leave them with as good an impression as possible, and to emphasise that you *do* want the job, even if, at that stage, you've decided that you don't (see below). Otherwise, they *may* believe that, despite your having been there and given an amazing performance, you could be attending a number of interviews and this was just another practice.

Still, if, after all, you think that this is *not* the job for you, or you couldn't work with that team, or you just don't like the environment – don't let it show. If you do, you're bound to leave a poor impression and it's worth considering that you may face the same interviewer again (possibly even in another company/role) or they may be asked by someone else about their opinion of you; or, crucially, they may come back to you with another position that suits you better. Do *not* burn your bridges!

Key Points to remember:

Enthusiasm and Energy – vital. More often than not, and to paraphrase Zig Zigler the American motivational speaker, "It's your Attitude rather than your Aptitude that gets results!"

What is the interviewer looking for? Relax, remain confident – and focused.

- Contribution: Can they contribute to the running / productivity / profitability of the company?

- Motivation: Will they really want to work hard for this organisation?

- Acceptability: Will they 'fit'?

Chapter 13
LinkedIn: A Brief Summary

For some time, LinkedIn's purpose has been misunderstood by a large proportion of potential users. LinkedIn is *not* simply another means whereby to 'hook up' with friends or colleagues. Rather, it's a platform on which anyone can join and liaise with people who, for whatever reason, might find you interesting, from a work perspective. Essentially, it's a networking platform for business people and it can be used for individual liaison as well as a means of contacting kindred spirits.

Hiring managers will often turn to your LinkedIn profile before even looking at your CV. I also know that LinkedIn can often play a strong part in the recruitment process: "Will this person fit? And do I actually like him/her?"

Whereas your CV will offer a totally dispassionate (if nonetheless accurate) résumé of your skills, experience and achievements, LinkedIn serves a different function: it illustrates the real you, although one should, essentially, complement the other.

You should be able to 'sell' yourself on LinkedIn – i.e., by making yourself attractive to others, because the skills and experience you offer could well be of interest to them. And you want these (relevant) people to connect with you, thus allowing you to develop a highly useful connection network. Consequently, anything you post on LinkedIn will be picked up by some, and then passed on to others... and possibly acted upon. It really is a most powerful medium.

Your profile will include the following key features:

1. **Your 'Headline':** a brief statement is fine, but also summarising your principal role(s), e.g., 'Strategy and Transformational Change Consultant, Interim Director, General Manager' – words or phrases that will be recognised by, for example, a Google search.

2. **Your photo:** Nothing too 'quirky' but a smiling 'head and shoulders', professionally done, is ideal.

Do *not* try to enhance your image in any way: photos from 20 years ago; 'cool' sunglasses that actually redact a third of your face anyway; you in a happy swimming group of four (or more...).

Otherwise, for them the reality, when they finally do meet you, could turn out to be a huge disappointment. You want the reader to say, "Yup – I'd be happy to meet this one."

3. **The About section:** This is where you describe what you do and why it might be *of interest to the reader*; a series of Q&As, for example:

'Looking for a senior NED role? I will help you to identify and exploit specific opportunities.'

And *always* in the first person. This is an informal way of setting out your professional stall and should be aimed at attracting the attention of others by: a) identifying their needs, then b) showing how you can meet them.

In other words, your LinkedIn profile can act as a quasi-website, offering your own skills and achievements in a way that might prove attractive to the reader (or, indeed, *their* contacts...)

4. **Experience:** Again, first person here and include an informal description of what

you've done. Achievements here are probably less relevant than on your CV – unless you'd personally saved your company £millions – but should also be written in terms that a layman would understand. In other words, esoteric jargon here is a complete waste of time.

5. Endorsements and Recommendations:
Endorsements are frills – nothing more really. However, it can definitely help if you can get one or two *recommendations*, preferably – but not essentially – from either a boss, former boss; existing or former client. Often totally unsolicited, surprisingly 99% of those you ask to write a recommendation for you will be happy to do so. It's true. And not only will it enhance your profile, but extracts from a recommendation can also be used to endorse what you've said in your CV 'Profile', thus giving it a greater air of credibility. For example:

'Mark was not only a key member of his team; he also led them to achieve truly excellent results for the company. I recommend him without question.' *[John Smith – CEO of Brown Consultant]*

Can be quite impressive...

Because LinkedIn is quite likely to be the 'go to' summary for someone interested in learning about you, it's vitally important to get these basic points absolutely spot on: Headline; Photo; About; Experience; Recommendations. People will judge you on it just as seriously as with your CV (perhaps even more so) and it does pay – particularly as a networking medium.

Chapter 14
Key aspects of a Great Presentation

The very thought of having to stand up for the first time in front of an audience of any size and then speak – interestingly – for a scheduled time, fills most people with total dread. But why?

Because unless you're supremely confident in your belief that you'll perform well, you'll probably be terrified: 'OMG – they'll think I'm rubbish!' is a common one but, again, why? They're *not* a hostile group of people; and yes, they do *want* you to shine! They really do. Who would want a new speaker to 'collapse' and struggle to keep their composure? However, anyone who's clearly nervous is always going to struggle.

But then your audience does want you to be good. They really would rather you didn't stumble on your words or appear so mind-numbingly nervous you can hardly speak. Nor would they take any pleasure in your public humiliation. No, they are your friends. And you should treat them accordingly. If you can do that, you're much more likely to be able to engage with them. Remember, the adage 'People employ *People*' can apply equally to presentations.

Having written your script, a good idea is first to pick it up, stand up and read it aloud[3], possibly to a trusted friend or partner. I *guarantee* – only then will you realise that you've either: repeated yourself three times; or that what you thought was a good sentence is actually a paragraph so long that its meaning has become totally... meaningless; or even that a certain line is just pure rubbish. Nerves, however, *will* play a part – the same sort of nervousness that you get before an important interview; except worse. It's the irrational belief that you're about to be closely scrutinised by people who, essentially, would rather you fail. And yet nothing could be further from the truth. (In either situation.)

Focus on three basic truths:

1. **Know your audience, and why they're there.** It's important to at least picture in your mind what they might want to learn - in other words not simply what *you* want

---

[3] This self-assessment example works for your written letters and CV as well.

to tell them – even to imagine what sort of questions they might ask. At this point, thorough research is crucial because that information can form an integral part not only of what you say to them, but that's clearly relevant to you and your presentation topic.

2. **Try to speak to and, where possible[4], make eye contact with each audience member at some point during your presentation.** Would you, in the audience, not be prepared to listen more closely to a speaker who has sought you out and made eye contact, however briefly? I think you would.

3. **Keep it simple.** As an audience member, it can be difficult to assimilate large tracts of information and figures, particularly from a PowerPoint presentation. Some may even nod off. (Sorry, but true.) Besides, it's been found that most audience members would usually prefer an expected 45-minute talk to finish after 30. Neat and simple. (No, they're not bored! Far from it. And most can't wait for the Q&A session...)

---

[4] Again, sheer audience numbers may influence your ability here...

You'll know that many stand-up comedians engage directly with audience members; indeed, it often forms an integral part of their act. If you were presenting to, say, a group of marketers, you might ask something like: 'OK, so who thinks that enforced deadlines can be an issue?' I should imagine that a few hands would go up and, by engaging directly with one or two about these specifics, the rest could well be drawn in to the chat because it's something upon which all would have an opinion at least and, suddenly, they're all keen to voice their views.

Indeed, it seems that a lively Q&A session will see one or two hands going up at first and, by the time it's finishing, you have a forest of raised arms. And whereas it's important to maintain your status within the room, so without allowing it to 'take over' the session, nonetheless this can often work well with a smaller audience, many of whom are delighted to engage directly with the speaker – and will talk about it afterwards in glowing terms.

I want you to imagine you're now in the audience, waiting to hear a presentation. If the speaker insists (and many do) on first telling you their name and then what they are about to talk about, you're already receiving redundant information and are possibly part way to switching off! But if their opening line had been, simply:

'Hello. I'd like to tell you a story…' you'd probably pay 100% attention. Why? Because, as with the interview techniques, just like children, we all like stories. Indeed, we much prefer them to a list of PowerPoint facts – and a well-told story, verbal illustration or series of stories, should include those facts anyway. If you can even make it mildly amusing – you'll have gained their attention – and will probably retain it throughout.

Incorporating these aspects of your presentation into a story form can be quite appealing. You'll also find that continuing your narrative from that point will be much easier, mainly because you'll feel that you've already engaged with your audience. They'll want to know what you have to say next.

Finally, if you do believe that giving your name to the audience is a vital part of the talk, do it at the end. Stand-up comedians will often sign off with it: "Well, thanks for being such a great audience! I've been Joe Smith. G'night!" By then, you should have already gained their attention and it's a good way to have them remember who the speaker was.

Chapter 15

A Flying Start

The new Job:

Anyone starting a new job will experience a range of emotions, which may include: interest, panic, fear, elation, contentment and satisfaction as they tentatively feel their way and possibly benefit from the goodwill of colleagues and bosses alike. During the next few weeks, the learning curve will, inevitably, flatten out as they begin to understand the role and its importance within the scheme of things. Some ideas of what to do:

- Do not panic!
- Introduce yourself to all team members and stakeholders. Ask as many questions as you can, and seek advice constantly (but avoiding becoming a nuisance).

- Set personal and job-related goals.

- Develop a good relationship with your boss by encouraging a dialogue between you.

- Establish an understanding of your mutual goals and targets.

- Review these regularly.

Starting a new job can be a daunting prospect, even for seasoned professionals. Although not always the case, your new employer may have a well-tried Induction Plan that will cover every-thing from 'Your Health & Safety in the Work-place', through computer systems and software processes to where the loos are. However, there's usually only one person who's *really* interested in how you progress: You. Consequently, you must be able to control your own induction.

You have the job description and employment contract, and so you'll be aware of the basics of what your new job requires of you. But there's much more to learn about how to become a 'valued member of the team', or possibly a manager. Whereas you should ask as many questions as you can, don't become a nuisance and start to establish what are the key aspects of the role, and what might be expected of you:

- Who are the important people in the organisation (and why)?

- What are the key functions of the team, and how is success measured, achieved – rewarded?

- Who are the key external stakeholders (or clients) and how do we ensure that their needs are met?

- Who's the office 'funny guy'?

- Where do we (or do we?) socialise after work?

The majority of your colleagues or team members will be more than happy to help you with all of these, so it's a good idea to set benchmarks as you settle into this new role e.g., one week; one month; three months, and have personal goals attached to each. You may want, after one week for example, to have introduced yourself to everyone in your team or to be totally familiar with the office layout. A three-month goal may be a mix of your own personal ambitions with those agreed with your manager. Many employers will have a three-month review anyway and you'll want to be able to monitor closely your own performance and how it appears to them.

Initiate a dialogue between you and your superiors as soon as possible and establish what, precisely, is expected of you, and how – possibly through a training regime – they can help you to achieve it. Starting with a good mutual understanding and performing as required, or even exceeding expectations, should lead to a positive relationship between you. (Without that dialogue, initiated by you, you're more likely to become simply another 'cog in the wheel'.)

There are definitely phases attached to a new job experience. After one week, when asked by friends, people will probably say something like: 'Yeah great! Lovely people, fun job...'. However, after three months: 'Yup, OK. People are great; I could be busier...' or perhaps not even as positive... The honeymoon is over and you're now simply another member of the team. You can guard against this 'middling' outcome by continually setting goals for yourself. Achieving them will not only bring your own satisfaction, but will set you up for the months that follow. After all, your job should be enjoyed, not endured.

Chapter 16

And, finally...

We live in an ever-changing world. Even during the time of my writing this book, we've experienced three Prime Ministers (and attendant Cabinet reshuffles), the variable effects of the Covid pandemic, lockdown and even the war in Ukraine. Another obvious example born out of the lockdown is the now almost universal acceptance of the so-called 'hybrid' remote working practice, as discussed in the Introduction to this book, one that seems likely to be with us for some time. Possibly forever...?

So – change is all around us in its various forms and we do seem able, in most cases, to adapt. But then we also tend to take for granted the many things that we can perform well enough in life without the need for extra coaching or tuition. We can manage life through a self-learning journey during which things we might regard as 'required but basic' skills will come to us naturally, either from constant repetition or simply through experience. Most of us can walk, run, even kick a ball without feeling we must turn to others for advice on the subject. However, why, when we're clearly petrified by the prospect of having to give a presentation to a group of people (of any number), writing our CV, or facing a particularly tricky interview, do we not seek help or guidance?

I wanted to illustrate how, if you adhere to a small number of basic principles, the process of tackling the writing of your CV or letter to performing a brilliant and memorable speech or presentation is never as daunting as it seems at first. Why? Because people do want you to be good and if you're able to adopt the principles of 'Keep it Simple, Stupid', you'll be astounded by how *simple* everything actually becomes.

For example, I was once given a set of shortened phrases which illustrated how our apparent need to over-fill sentences with 'verbiage' can be simplified – to great effect:

A

Macbeth was very ambitious. This led him to wish to become king of Scotland. The witches told him that this wish of his would come true. However, the King of Scotland at that time was Duncan. Encouraged by his wife, Macbeth murdered Duncan. He was thus able to succeed Duncan as king.

(55 words.)

B

Encouraged by his wife, Macbeth achieved his ambition and realised the prediction of the witches by murdering Duncan and becoming King of Scotland in his place.

(26 words.)

I do try to live by a simplified code but, like everyone, often fail to do so. But this illustration sums up my credo and the guidelines I use in everything I do. If you can start writing a cover letter or even a full presentation whilst thinking throughout what the reader or audience *really* wants to read or hear, you will have made a success of it.

Acknowledgements

Having discovered very early on that writing this book was going to involve much more input from me than I had thought, it was made so much easier by the support and encouragement I received from others. Key among them was Indie Authors World's Kim McLeod and Rachel Hessin who were not only both fantastic with their guidance and patience with my initial fumblings, but also with the continuing tasks that need attention.

Writing this book was made so much easier by the support and encouragement I received from others, principal among whom I'd definitely mention are: my in-laws, Jonathan Meuli & Liffy Grant – both of whom offered huge help with proofreading and copy-editing; Mark Jackson of www.MKJPhotography.co.uk who produced some outstanding photographs; dear Georgina Hart – www.georgina-hart.co.uk – for her patience and understanding of what I wanted with her amazing cartoons. I must also thank Miles Duncan for all his guidance on LinkedIn over the past four years, and Gin Lalli (www.ginlalli.com) and Dr.Laura Wyness (www.laurawyness.com) who, being published authors themselves, were able to provide me with much-needed guidance and helpful ideas; and Eloise Leeson (ww.olim.com) for her great support and wise words.

About the Author

After 25 years working in senior sales and business management within two farm equipment distributorships, Sandy decided to shift careers to a sector he loved – recruitment. Sandy has been  working as a freelancer in financial recruitment, career management and communication for more than 24 years.

Sandy's experience has made him a household name as a career coach and communication specialist, especially in Edinburgh. He has helped many people to further their work aspirations and transform their career, developing skills they can revisit throughout their life.

Sandy's professional, humorous and welcoming personality is a key strength that allows him to warmly connect with clients. This is reflected in the outstanding praise for Sandy and his services that can be viewed at the front of this book or on Sandy's LinkedIn page.

His love of helping people to build the confidence and skills they need to have a successful career have taken him beyond 'retirement'. So, for the first time Sandy has shared his passion and knowledge in this book, developing a new range of skills of his own in the process. Proving his own teachings that you are never too old to learn.

Sandy would be delighted to connect with you on: LinkedIn https://www.linkedin.com/in/sandycullen/